READING THE BOOK

A POPULAR ESSAY ON CHRISTIAN BIBLICAL HERMENEUTICS

JOSEPH FRANKOVIC

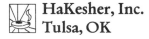 HaKesher, Inc.
Tulsa, OK

Copyright © 1997 by Joseph Frankovic
Published by HaKesher, Inc.
9939 S. 71st East Avenue
Tulsa, OK 74133-5338
Telephone & FAX: 918-298-8816
E-Mail: hakesher@aol.com
Internet: www.hakesher.org

First Printing September 1997

Cover photo by Don Wheeler
Cover design by Jerry Nabors
Printed by Western Printing Company, Inc.
in the United States of America

Typeset in Garamond
by Kenneth R. Mullican, Jr.

Library of Congress Catalog Card Number
97-75100

ISBN 1-891341-00-6

This essay is dedicated to
my teacher and friend, Professor Burt Visotzky,
who taught me how to read the Book.

עשה לך רב וקנה לך חבר

TABLE OF CONTENTS

PREFACE

Reading the Book was conceived in Jerusalem, Israel. On May 25, 1996 the basic idea of a *Jesus-centric* approach to reading the Bible was presented at the Narkis Street Congregation's weekly Shabat Bible study. That particular morning we arranged the study around a panel discussion. In addition to myself, Brad Young, David Bivin, and Halvor Ronning participated on the panel. The favorable response from the audience encouraged me to continue supplementing and refining the material.

Later that year Derek White invited me to be a plenary speaker at the biannual Christian Friends of Israel (CFI) conference held at Ashburnham Place near Battle in East Sussex, England. Again the audience responded favorably to the presentation. At the close of the conference, Mr. White suggested that CFI transcribe the audio cassette of *Reading the Book* and publish it. I agreed, and he, along with others at CFI, invested long hours in transcribing and making corrections to the manuscript. When the British version of *Reading the Book* is published, it will carry the title *Re-Reading the Book*.

In the United States, I continued to supplement and revise CFI's transcribed text. The American version contains a considerable amount of additional material and has a higher level of readability. Ken and Lenore Mullican of HaKesher, Inc. kindly agreed to publish the new version.

Reading the Book originated as a transcription of a lecture intended for an audience of well-read and motivated lay people. I have tried to make the text as readable as possible without recourse to rewriting it from scratch. Despite my efforts, I am aware that *Reading the Book* still exhibits vestiges of its origin as an oral presentation.

Lastly, I must mention that the title *Reading the Book* is not my own. In 1991, my doctoral mentor Professor Burt Visotzky wrote a popular book as an introduction to rabbinic methods of biblical interpretation, otherwise known as midrash. He entitled it *Reading the Book: Making the Bible a Timeless Text.* (Happily, this fine little book will soon be republished.) *Reading the Book* seemed like the right title for my essay, too. In fact, that is what I named the Bible study back in May of 1996. With Professor Visotzky's permission, I have retained that title for the American version published by HaKesher, Inc.

Joseph Frankovic
Wichita Falls, Texas
September 1997

FOREWORD

In his book published over three decades ago, A. Berkeley Mickelsen stated that the task of scholars who wish to interpret the Bible is "to find out the meaning of a statement (command, question) for the author and for the first hearers or readers, and thereupon to transmit that meaning to modern readers."[1] He then set down a series of principles by which this could be achieved. More recently many biblical scholars have been critical of this approach and question whether it is possible to determine what the original author meant. They suggest that the "authorial intention is irretrievable, or irrelevant to the interpretive process altogether."[2]

Two basic emphases can be found in current works on hermeneutics. Source criticism, form criticism, tradition-historical criticism, and redaction criticism fall into a group which is diachronic (they trace the text through time) and makes use of historical, archaeological, and literary backgrounds. This is often called the historical-critical method, and it has been judged as sterile by many. The other group includes structuralist criticism, narrative criticism, and reader-response criticism. These put stress on the final form of the text, the relationship between various textual elements, and the interactions between texts and readers. These are part of the reader-response method and are

---

[1]A. Berkeley Mickelsen. *Interpreting the Bible* (Grand Rapids: Eerdmans, 1963), p. 5.

[2]Stephen R. Haynes and Steven L. McKenzie, eds. *To Each Its Own Meaning: An Introduction to Biblical Criticisms and their Application* (Louisville: Westminster/John Knox Press, 1993), p. 3.

often seen as reactionary to the historical-critical method. Kaiser and Silva suggest a third emphasis which they call the syntactical-theological method. They claim that this "is holistic in involving both historical and practical applications."[3]

The non-specialist looks at these various approaches and wonders how there can be so many different meanings to a biblical passage. If the scholars cannot agree, what chance does a layman have for correctly handling the Word of Truth? Many leaders and pastors in the Charismatic movement have had no formal training. They depend more often on the "work of the Holy Spirit" to illumine the mind to the correct interpretation of Scripture. But even here there are many different interpretations. Is the Holy Spirit divided? Is He not able to convey the truth to all, or at least to a majority, of believers?

Kaiser and Silva point out that "the question of relevancy has taken precedence over the question of 'What does the text mean?'" They argue that so much emphasis has been put on individual freedom that the primary question is no longer, "Is it true?" but rather "Does it matter?"[4]

Joseph Frankovic has recognized the difficulty that modern readers face in the interpretation of the text. He contends that "interpreting the Bible is a question of acute relevance, because how we understand Scripture ultimately determines to a large degree how we put it into practice." And, of course, as Evangelical Christians we are concerned

---

[3]Walter C. Kaiser and Moises Silva. *An Introduction to Biblical Hermeneutics: The Search for Meaning* (Grand Rapids: Zondervan, 1994), p. 26.

[4]Ibid. p. 10.

with making it practical in our daily lives. Several illustrations are given to show how various interpretations can be reached depending on our presuppositions. These presuppositions are the different pairs of glasses that we may use in reading the text.

A major contribution that the author makes is calling our attention to the fact that much of the New Testament does not flow directly from the Old Testament. Several hundred years of time, radical shifts in culture because of the dominant ruling powers, and significant changes in theology followed the close of the Old Testament. The *milieu* into which Jesus was born was quite different from what it was in the Old Testament. Jesus was a part of Second Temple Judaism. Thus, the interpreter of the Word should be aware that other factors need to be considered in addition to the Old Testament. The teaching method of Jesus is closely related to the midrashic approach of the first century A.D.

Another area of interest cited by the author is the change of audience addressed by the writers of the New Testament from one that is Jewish to one that is primarily non-Jewish. The target culture changed. This change made a difference in the emphasis given to the text. The author suggests that perhaps this new culture has received too much emphasis in our exegesis, and more attention should be given to the source culture, the Second Temple Judaism of the land of Israel, a Judaism that had great diversity. At the same time we must be aware that the New Testament is a collection of books, and each needs to be approached according to its literary genre. The problem of the chronological sequence of the Gospels is clearly stated, and a possible solution is given.

The approach the author wishes us to consider is what he calls *Jesus-centric*. You may not agree with everything presented, but after reading it I believe you will have a better understanding of Jesus and how he influences the interpretation of the New Testament, and to a great extent the Old Testament as well.

Roy E. Hayden
Professor of Old Testament
Graduate School of Theology
Oral Roberts University
Tulsa, Oklahoma

Acknowledgments

From the inception of this project in Jerusalem, Israel, through its intermediate stages in the United Kingdom and Wichita Falls, Texas, to its completion in Tulsa, Oklahoma, many individuals have encouraged and assisted me in ways both large and small. Their names I have listed below, and to each of them I extend a warm thank you.

*Ahrens, Erwin &
Patricia*
Alley, Gary
Anthony, John & Connie
Ashdown, Jennifer
Bean, William & Trish
Bivin, David & Josa
Bouwmeester, Augustus
Chambers, Barbara
Cook, Allan
Cornell, John & Alleen
Cox, Chad & Debbie
*Dampier, Dennis, Jean &
Cecilia*
Davis, Chris & Adora
Davidson, Eliyad & Vera
Davis, Bob
Dorr, John & Debbie
Fields, Weston & DeWitt
Flusser, David
Forbes, David & Jenny
*Frankovic, Janet &
Theresa*

Frye, Pete & Dawn
Gillespie, Judith
Greenburg, Lisa
Haccius, Ann
Hadley, Bob & Nancy
Hall, Mark
Hartley, John
Hayden, Roy & Mary
Henley, Richard
Hussini, Haldun
Jaye, Timothy & Sheryl
Jeter, John & Billye
Kanitz, Lori
Kern, James & Lynne
Knight, Tim & Maggie
Kvasnica, Brian
*Kopp, Charles &
Elizabeth*
Lawrence, John & Dawn
Lindsey, Margaret
Maxwell, Desi
Miller, Mike
Mullican, Ken & Lenore

Mullican, Kenny & Stephanie
Niems, Jeff, Debbie & Barbara
Nolting, Annette
Notley, Steve & Sunya
Opittek, Ruth
Petkelis, Tony & Wawanna
Pittaway, John & Kim
Poirier, Jack & Missy
Polinski, John & Pat
Pryor, Dwight & Jeanette
Pileggi, David & Carol
Purcell, Dick & Joan
Purnell, Martin
Ray, Joseph & Kay
Ronning, Halvor & Mariam
Schwieterman, Kip
Seegerst, Else
Severn, John & Katrina
Solomon, Nathan
Schwartz, Lisa
Tofsar, Dubi
Twena, Helen
Visotzky, Burt
Vos, Joseph
White, Derek
Wright, Archie
Young, Brad

INTRODUCTION

The challenges, difficulties, and risks of biblical interpretation remain with us whether we are willing to acknowledge them or not. Choosing to ignore them, we can pretend that they are irrelevant. Ignoring them, however, is a response by default. On the other hand, by acknowledging these challenges, difficulties and risks, we can engage them head-on and strive to find workable solutions for reading the Book.

I am not promoting my solution as being the only right answer. Rather I offer it as a fresh approach for helping us to become more effective readers, preachers, and teachers of the Bible.

A SURVEY OF WAYS
TO READ SCRIPTURE

Our discussion commences with Malachi 4:5:

"Behold, I am going to send you Elijah the prophet before the coming of the great and terrible day of the Lord."

Notice the verb "coming." John the Baptist alluded to this verb in Malachi 4:5, when he asked Jesus through the agency of two followers whether or not he was "The Coming One" (Matthew 11:2, 3).

In certain streams of ancient Jewish thought this verb contributed to a cluster of ideas that drew imagery from the motifs of the Son of Man and separation (as a metaphor for judgment; cf. Daniel 7:13 and John 5:27). If we are to think more like the ancient Jews before whom Jesus sat as a teacher, we should initially think of judgment when, in the synoptic gospels, we encounter the verb "coming" in combination with the title "Son of Man" or the imagery of separation. This cluster of ideas finds clear expression in Matthew 25:31-46.

What then was the significance of John's question in Matthew 11:2? Was John merely asking Jesus if he were indeed the Christ? Perhaps John was not asking a question, but telling Jesus something with a question. He may have been prodding Jesus to conduct himself in a manner consistent with his Messianic expectations. John had been preaching at the river Jordan that "his winnowing fork is in his hand" and "the axe is laid at the root" (Matthew 3:10, 12). Jesus, however, preached Isaiah 61:1-2 as the opening sermon of his public ministry:

> *The Spirit of the Lord God is upon Me, because He anointed me to preach the gospel to the poor. He has sent me to proclaim release to the captives, and recovery of sight to the blind, to set free those who are downtrodden, to proclaim the favorable year of the Lord* (Luke 4:18, 19)—period!

Jesus stopped reading in the middle of Isaiah 61:2, immediately before the phrase, "and the day of vengeance of our God." Jesus' abrupt stop at that point seems to have been no mere coincidence. This becomes more apparent in light of the fact that he reiterated the same points of this sermon as he instructed John's two messengers to tell John what they had heard and seen (Matthew 11:4-6).

I want to underscore the difference of opinion regarding the Messianic task which existed between Jesus and John. In order to represent their respective views, I will put on different pairs of eyeglasses. First, I will wear my John the Baptist spectacles. When wearing these glasses, I read the Bible like John the Baptist. How did John understand Malachi 4:5? He likely was aware that others saw him as fulfilling the role of this Elijah-like herald (cf. Luke 1:16, 17). How then did he read Malachi 4:5? John apparently thought that God would send this herald immediately prior to or at the advent of the great and terrible day of the Lord (i.e., the day of judgment)!

John's reading of the text had far-reaching ramifications for the way he conducted his ministry. In fact, his understanding of this verse, and of others related to it, helped motivate him to send the two messengers to prod Jesus with the question: "Are you The One Who Comes, or shall we look for another?" (Matthew 11:3). What John may have been saying to Jesus was, "Why are you not ushering in judgment according to my expectations?" Jesus, in John's thinking, already stood with a winnowing fork in hand. The axe had already fallen. These phrases are metaphors for judgment.

Now, I will put on my Jesus spectacles and read the text again. How did Jesus understand Malachi 4:5? Elijah will come before the day of the Lord, but there will be an intermediate span of time (lasting potentially thousands of years) of grace, redemption, and healing. Jesus referred to the advent of this special time or age in Matthew 11:12 as the breaking forth of the Kingdom of Heaven (note the NIV translation of that verse).

Jesus and John read Malachi 4:5 in two very different ways. How wide the gap and how significant the ramifications in light of how each man conducted his public ministry. Moreover, John's understanding of the verse is closer to the *peshat*, that is, the plain grammatical meaning of the verse. Jesus' interpretation, on the other hand, can only be achieved by reading Malachi 4:5 as part of a greater complex of verses.

Reading the text is the crux of the matter. That is one point that I intend to highlight throughout this short essay. Interpreting the Bible is a question of acute relevance because how we understand Scripture ultimately determines to a large degree how we put it into practice.

Consider a second example. Malachi 3:10 is a well-known verse, one which we hear regularly in American churches, moments before the morning offertory:

> *"Bring the whole tithe into the storehouse, so that there may be food in My house, and test me now in this," says the Lord of Hosts, "if I will not open for*

*you the windows of heaven, and pour out for you a
blessing until it overflows."*

I recently asked a woman what this verse meant.
She replied, "If a person seeks God's kingdom and pays
tithes regularly, God will meet that person's needs."
What she said is an acceptable interpretation. If we are
faithful in paying our tithes to our local church, then
God will ensure that our financial needs are met. (I
have narrowed down the range of meaning of her expla-
nation for the purpose of this discussion.) This kind
woman more or less repeated a standard Protestant understanding of the verse.

Let us now read Malachi 3:10 with the assistance of
rabbinic spectacles. How do the Rabbis understand the
nature of this blessing "without measure?" Rain! In
fact, the Hebrew phrase "windows of heaven" is used in
Genesis 7:11 where God said that he opened the windows of heaven, and it poured. We find also that the
verb in the phrase "empty upon you a blessing" is the
same verb which appears in Ecclesiastes 11:3 for rain
pouring down. Anybody who has lived in Israel knows
the vital role the autumn and spring rains play in that
region. Moreover, the continuation of the passage in
Malachi supports the rabbinic reading of this text.[1]

Cultural and religious orientation has influenced our
present-day reading of this verse. We interpret it within
a defined preaching and teaching tradition. This molds
our understanding of the verse. Malachi 3:10 is a good

---

[1] *Metsudat Tsion* on Malachi 3:10; cf. *Talmud Bavli* 22b where
Malachi 3:10 is cited in a discussion about the delicate dilemma of
praying for rain to stop when God gives too much rainfall (i.e.,
too much of a good thing).

example of a passage onto which we have loaded baggage. The simple meaning of Malachi 3:10 is that God will grant abundant rainfall.

I am not saying that the baggage we have loaded onto this verse is unwarranted. I merely want to point out that it is there. My remarks here are not intended to be judgmental. From studying midrashic methods of biblical exegesis, I have learned to be more tolerant of competing interpretations, because midrash takes the view that the more meanings which can be squeezed from a verse, the better.

Consider a final example from Matthew 16:13-19, Peter's confession about Jesus: Jesus asked, *"Who do you say that I am?"*, and Peter answered, *"Thou art the Christ, the Son of the living God."* To that Jesus replied, *"Blessed are you Simon Bar-Jonah, because flesh and blood did not reveal this to you . . . . And I also say to you that you are Peter, and upon this rock I will build my church . . . ."*

Starting with papal spectacles, I will read this passage from a Catholic perspective. Wearing these spectacles, I interpret Jesus' words as a precedent for papal succession. The implications are obvious, and if others cannot see them, they must work at relinquishing their Protestant tendentiousness. (Matthew 16:18 is one verse which is cited for supporting the tradition of papal succession).

Now I shall put on Protestant-Evangelical spectacles. Wearing these spectacles, I see that this text does *not* mean that Peter is the Rock. Rather, the rock is his confession— the truth, the correctness, the rightness of that confession. This is the rock upon which Jesus builds his Church. To say otherwise is a distortion of the Word of God.

We have unfairly ignored a third perspective. As an alumnus of Oral Roberts University, I am uniquely qualified to give the Charismatic reading: *"And I also say to you that you are Peter, and upon this rock"* then jump down as soon as possible to *"I will give you the keys of the kingdom of heaven; and whatever you shall bind on earth shall be bound in heaven . . . ."* There we have it. The Charismatic reading zeroes in on the binding and loosing of verse 19. What comes before and after is merely detail.

In the ancient Jewish literature one finds a parable about God looking for an individual upon whom he can build. Though the parable is found in a late midrashic collection, I am inclined to think that this parable contains an exceptional example of an early tradition which has survived and found expression in a late text. The parable actually preserves in the Hebrew the Greek word *petra*, which had been absorbed into Mishnaic Hebrew. The parable offers a delightfully imaginative glimpse of God searching for a faithful, stable individual upon whom he can rely.

> *In the same manner, the Holy One, blessed is he, before he created the world, sat and examined the generation of Enosh and the generation of the Flood. "How can I create the world when those wicked people will appear and provoke me to anger?" he said. When, however, the Holy One, blessed is he, saw Abraham, he said, "Here I have found solid rock (petra) on which I can build and upon which I can lay the world's foundations."* [2]

---

[2] *Yalkut Shim'oni* on Numbers 23:9. The English translation was done by David Bivin and used with his permission. For a

For the rabbis, the solid rock was Abraham, but for Jesus, it had become Peter. In the light of this parable, parallels from the Qumran Scrolls,[3] and an emendation suggested by Professor Shmuel Safrai to read a Tannaitic passage as "Abraham the cornerstone" instead of "Abraham at the corner,"[4] I am convinced that Peter is the rock, the foundation upon which Jesus intended to build.

Please do not construe my conclusion to indicate that I view Matthew 16:18 as proof for papal succession. Nevertheless, based upon a comparative approach with an ancient Jewish parable, it seems that by making a pun on Peter's name and the word *petra*, Jesus called him something equivalent in English to "Rocky" and said, "Upon this rock I will build."

Could the Protestant Evangelical interpretation be a response to the Catholic interpretation? Are reactionary motives ideal motives for interpreting the Bible? Evangelicals tend to read this passage to some degree in a manner that responds to the Catholic position.

Matthew 16:13-19 serves as another example that demonstrates the relevance of the issue of biblical interpretation—how we read the Bible results in interpretation, which ultimately affects practice. This is the main point which I want to convey in our survey of ways to read Malachi 4:5, Malachi 3:10, and Matthew 16:18.

Hebrew text of the parable, see *Yalkut Shim'oni 'al HaTorah* (Jerusalem: Mossad Harav Kook, 1986), pp. 487, 488.

[3]See Menahem Kister, "Plucking on the Sabbath and Christian-Jewish Polemic," *Immanuel* 24 & 25 (1990), pp. 35, 36.

[4]David Bivin, "Matthew 16:18: The *Petros-petra* Wordplay—Greek, Aramaic, or Hebrew?" *Jerusalem Perspective* 46 & 47 (Sept.-Dec. 1994), p. 36.

TRANSLATION, INTERPRETATION, AND BENDING THE TEXT

First year seminary students quickly learn the meaning of the words exegesis and eisegesis. Exegesis is borrowed from Greek and means "to lead out." Eisegesis is also borrowed from Greek and means "to lead into." Ideally, seminarians are taught to exegete a text (i.e., to lead the meaning out of a text). What we lead out of a text, however, is governed by what we have led into it beforehand. The distinction between exegesis and eisegesis is not always as rigid and well-defined as we suppose.

Another word about which seminarians often talk is hermeneutics. Hermeneutics comes from the Greek word *hermeneutikos*. The Greek verb from the same root means "to translate" and "to interpret."[5] Interestingly, the ancients did not make a clear distinction between translation and interpretation. Only moderns make this clear-cut distinction. In reality, a translation is an interpretation. It could be argued that an English version of the Bible is as much a commentary as it is a translation.[6]

---

[5]See Walter Bauer, William Arndt, and Wilbur Gingrich, *A Greek-English Lexicon of the New Testament and Other Early Christian Literature*, 2nd rev. and augmented ed. (Chicago: University of Chicago, 1979), p. 310. See also the Mishnaic Hebrew word *Targum* in Marcus Jastrow, *A Dictionary of the Targumim, The Talmud Babli and Yerushalmi, and the Midrashic Literature* (Jerusalem: Horev, n.d.), p. 1695.

[6]In the second century A.D., R. Judah the Patriarch had already addressed this dilemma for translators with his pointed comment:

Every reader or community of faith interprets or bends the biblical text. This is neither inherently devious nor wrong. Every reader who comes to the biblical text bends it in one direction or another. Every community of faith supports and defends its doctrines and guidelines for praxis with an appeal to Scripture.

Do we not do the same thing? We cite scriptural precedent for the things we do. We read the text in a way which affirms and promotes our particular mode of Christian behavior. Distinct communities of faith must do that. Bending the text is necessary in order to ensure the Bible's relevance in the life of the community, regardless of whether that community is Jewish, Catholic, or Protestant.

Charismatics and Evangelicals also bend the text. All of us do it, and we should not be embarrassed or reluctant to acknowledge that we bend it. One way that we bend Scripture is with homiletical license. Have you ever heard a good sermon and thought, "I have never read that verse that way!"? The reason may have been homiletical license. The preacher expounded the text

---

"The one who literally translates a verse of Scripture is a counterfeiter, whereas the one who translates it dynamically is a blasphemer." For a Hebrew text of R. Judah's comment, see *Megilla* 3(4):41 in *The Tosefta, The Order of Mo'ed,* ed. Saul Lieberman (Jerusalem: Jewish Theological Seminary of America, 1992), p. 364. Note also *Jewish Antiquities* 1:5, 17 where Josephus claimed to be recording in Greek a precise account of Israel's history translated from the Hebrew Scriptures, but according to modern standards, produced a free, paraphrastic retelling of the biblical narrative. For an English translation, see Josephus, v. 4 in *The Loeb Classical Library*, trans. H. St. J. Thackeray (Cambridge, MA: Harvard, 1961), pp. 5, 9.

in an innovative way. He or she bent the text, but within the parameters of an accepted preaching tradition.

What about study notes in English translations of the Bible? There is a well-known Bible called the Scofield Reference Bible and, for some Christians in the United States, its notes have assumed a status of near inerrancy. I do not know precisely how influential the Scofield Reference Bible has been; however, to say that Cyrus Ingerson Scofield has had an enduring influence on Protestant-Evangelical thinking is not an overstatement. Scofield bent the text in a certain way. He created a paradigm for reading the Bible which many still embrace. Similar though less pronounced claims could be made for *The NIV Study Bible*. I imagine that some reading this essay, having consulted the notes in *The NIV Study Bible* on one occasion or another, have questioned the author's perspective.

All of us bend or stretch the text. It must be done in order to ensure that the Bible remains applicable to the ever changing circumstances and needs of the community of faith. Bending Scripture also helps make the Word of God come alive in the minds and hearts of the laity. In order to preach and teach, we must engage in interpretation. Yet once interpretation and exposition begin, we have begun bending the biblical text, hopefully, with good intentions and in an edifying direction.

11

THE CHALLENGE

Having laid the groundwork above, I now want to ask: Did Jesus read, preach, and teach his Bible like a Catholic? Did he read, preach, and teach his Bible like a Lutheran? Like a Methodist? Like an Evangelical? So, we see the challenge, and I think most of us are aware of this challenge, namely that there is a gap between the way Jesus read, preached, and taught his Bible and the way we read, preach, and teach our Bible.

While we cannot reproduce the approach of Jesus to his text, we can make good progress toward entering into Jesus' conceptual world and by doing so, reduce the gap between his reading and our reading of the Bible. Through serious, diligent comparative study of the synoptic gospels with other ancient Jewish sources, we can advance toward bringing our reading, preaching, and teaching of the Bible more into line with his.[7]

---

[7]Marvin Wilson has addressed the dilemma of "a Western world with an Eastern book." In his discussion, he has included two provoking quotations. The first originates from Bishop John Spong: "If the Bible is going to be understood in our day, we must develop 'Hebrew eyes' and 'Hebrew attitudes' toward life." The second comes from the writings of the renowned Swiss theologian Karl Barth: "The Bible . . . is a Jewish book. It cannot be read and understood and expounded unless we are prepared to become Jews with the Jews." Marvin R. Wilson, *Our Father Abraham: Jewish Roots of the Christian Faith* (Grand Rapids/Dayton: Eerdmans/Center for Judaic-Christian Studies, 1989), p. 24. In our day, while many serious, well-intentioned Christians would agree with Wilson, the challenge remains to motivate them to work toward the necessary changes in thought, attitudes, and education which Spong and Barth's statements require.

ANCIENT WRITERS
AND MODERN READERS

Allow me to pursue some thoughts on issues of biblical interpretation which mainly arise from the temporal and cultural distances between us and the writers and original readers of the New Testament. As a starting point, we will consider something Professor David Flusser wrote in his *Judaism and the Origins of Christianity*. As is evident from the table of contents, Flusser has devoted much of his academic career to studying Jesus. He is regarded as Israel's leading authority on nascent Christianity. This is what he wrote:

> *It has been largely forgotten by Christian scholars and believers that the New Testament is not a direct heir of the religious and moral attitude of the Old Testament. Between the compilation of the Old Testament and the time of Jesus, many centuries elapsed and the very nature of the Jewish approach to God and man had been transformed. Christianity arose on the basis of these fresh new Jewish achievements.*[8]

Can we identify some examples of these fresh Jewish achievements from the inter-testamental period which are reflected in the New Testament? Is the phrase Kingdom of Heaven found in the Old Testament? It

---

[8]David Flusser, *Judaism and the Origins of Christianity* (Jerusalem: Magnes Press, 1988), p. xvi, xvii. The eminent Christian scholar, R. H. Charles penned similar thoughts over eighty years ago. See R. H. Charles, *Religious Development Between the Old and the New Testament* (London: Williams and Norgate, 1914), pp. 7-11.

does not appear there, but when reading Jesus' teachings, we find that it has already become almost a technical term. The sages, and the rabbis who came after them, read back into the Torah—the five books of Moses—that the Kingdom of Heaven first became manifest in history at the parting of the Red Sea.

Overwhelmed by what God had done, Moses and the people burst into a song of praise and thanksgiving, which is recorded in Exodus 15:1-18. The last line of that song says, *"The Lord reigns forever and ever"* (cf. Exodus 15:18 in the LXX). Though not attracting much attention in Christian preaching and teaching,[9] this verse apparently assumed a place of prominence in Jewish theology prior to the advent of Christianity. For the sages of Israel, and the rabbis who came after them, the parting of the Red Sea marked the first place in history where the Kingdom of Heaven appeared. The idea is articulated clearly in a prayer recited Friday evenings in synagogue by faithful Jews:

> *Your Kingdom your sons saw as you peeled back the sea before Moses. The people responded, 'This is my God!' and they said, 'The Lord reigns forever and ever.'* [10]

When we encounter the phrase "Kingdom of Heaven" or its sister expression "Kingdom of God" in

---

[9]The Septuagint translation of Exodus 15:18 and early rabbinic comments on the same verse play a significant role in helping modern expositors grasp Jesus' conception of the Kingdom of Heaven. Yet a study Bible as widely acclaimed as *The NIV Study Bible* offers no comment on Exodus 15:18.

[10]For a Hebrew text of this prayer and an alternative English translation, see Joseph Hertz, trans. and ed., *The Authorized Daily Prayer Book,* rev. ed. (New York: Bloch, 1985), pp. 370, 371.

Jesus' teachings, we should form a mental image of God's redemptive power being manifested in the presence of his people. This cluster of ideas and imagery concerning the Kingdom of Heaven is one of the fresh achievements of post-biblical, Second Temple-period Judaism.

What about parables? In the Old Testament, we can find primitive or prototypical forms of the parable. But these do not approach in complexity and sophistication the level achieved by the synoptic parables. The emergence of the classical form of the parable involving the king, the father, the steward, the servant, or the son belongs to these fresh achievements of Judaism between the two Testaments.

One of Jesus' roles in his earthly ministry--not his only role but one of them--was that of a prophet. He went to Jerusalem to prophesy against the corrupt aristocratic priests who administrated the temple. If Jesus functioned as a prophet, why did he not use the phrase, "Thus says the Lord"? The concept of a prophet had evolved. Jesus did not need to use the Old Testament expression, "Thus says the Lord," to be recognized as a prophet.

I have pointed to three examples of post-biblical Judaism's fresh achievements. Others could be given, but space limits me to these three striking examples. While not exhaustive, they are nevertheless representative of a large corpus of material which we cannot explore here.

Christianity arose on the basis of these developments in inter-testamental Judaism. Jesus was an organic part of post-biblical, late Second Temple Judaism, which had evolved into something distinct from Old Testament Judaism.

This presents a big challenge because too often when training pastors in seminary, we assume that by studying the Old Testament we have covered the Jewish background to the New Testament. This represents a first step. Obtaining an excellent command of the Old Testament is invaluable for helping us to understand the New Testament, but it is only the initial, most fundamental step. We must add to that first step and study these fresh achievements that occurred in between the Old and New Testaments. This point has momentous implications for developing seminary curricula, and the way we equip future pastors to interpret Jesus' teachings. All this determines the way the Bible is preached from our pulpits, and in the end it influences the way the person sitting in the pew puts the text into practice. A lot is at stake here.

A second consideration is that Jesus lived in the land of Israel in the first century A.D. In the land of Israel a way of reading Scripture known as *midrash* emerged. One way to define midrash is to say that it was a strategy, system, or method of interpretation that the sages of Israel pioneered in order to keep the biblical text in currency among the people.

About two centuries after the Jews had returned from Babylon under Persian rule, they faced Alexander the Great's victorious army. The subsequent introduction of Hellenism into the Levant reshaped Judaism in a spectacular way. Judaism's response to Hellenism included the development of midrash. The sages had to find a way to keep Judaism meaningful and flexible enough to adapt to the new circumstances.

The arrival of Alexander meant that more than a new government had come to rule. The conquered peoples of the Near East were impressed by Hellenistic culture. Its appeal attracted many to embrace its ways. Moreover, the Greeks, and the Romans after them, were proud purveyors of their cultural achievements.

Although Hellenistic influences seeped deeply into ancient Judaism, the sages made efforts to resist certain aspects of the foreign culture. Tensions sometimes escalated. Jerusalem became a vortex of divergent cultural, social, political, and religious perspectives. In fact, Eastern and Western culture actually met each other on the coastal plain, which runs north and south about twenty miles west of Jerusalem. Heading east from the coastal plain, away from the Mediterranean commercial traffic, and going up into the hill country, one began the transition from Western to predominantly Eastern culture.

Within the borders of Israel, the biblical, Jewish approach to God and man clashed with Greco-Roman paganism. P. V. N. Myers expressed succinctly the basic source of the tension when he described Roman power reaching Judea in 63 B.C. Entering the Holy of Holies, against the protests of the High Priest, Pompey discovered nothing but a dark chamber with a small chest holding some sacred relics placed at its center. In Myers' words, "The Romans here for the first time came in direct contact with a people whose ideas of God and of life they were wholly incapable of understanding."[11]

---

[11]Philip Van Ness Myers, *Rome: Its Rise and Fall*, 2nd ed. (Boston: Ginn and Company, 1901), p. 281. James Parkes expressed a similar thought in these words, "The adjustment of a monotheistic people to a polytheistic world was not an easy one." James Parkes, *The Conflict of the Church and the Synagogue* (New York: Atheneum, 1969), p. 371.

Welcoming and even Judaizing some aspects of Hellenistic culture[12] but rejecting others, the sages and rabbis developed midrash as a strategy to maintain Judaism's relevancy in the face of the pressing issues of their day.

---

[12]See S. Stein, "The Influence of Symposia Literature on the Literary Form of the Pesah Haggadah," *Journal of Jewish Studies*, 8 (1957), pp. 13-44. Note David Daube's assessment of the mixing of Hellenistic and Jewish cultural elements which he offered in a discussion of the historical origins and development of Talmudic law: ". . . when the Hellenistic methods were first adopted, about 100 to 25 B.C., the 'classical,' Tannaitic era of Rabbinic law was just opening. That is to say, the borrowing took place in the best period of Talmudic jurisprudence, when the Rabbis were masters, not slaves, of the new influences. The methods taken over were thoroughly hebraized in spirit as well as form, adapted to the native material, worked out so as to assist the natural progress of Jewish law." David Daube, "Rabbinic Methods of Interpretation and Hellenistic Rhetoric," *Hebrew Union College Annual* 22 (1949), p. 240. See also, Saul Lieberman, *Greek in Jewish Palestine* (New York: The Jewish Theological Seminary of America, 1994), pp. 20, 21. Not mincing words on this subject, Burton Visotzky has written, ". . . the rabbis were Hellenists, much as were the Church Fathers." Burton Visotzky, *Fathers of the World: Essays in Rabbinic and Patristic Literatures* (Tübingen: J. C. B. Mohr, 1995), p. 2. His remark certainly underscores one side of the rabbis' biculturalism. One cannot fairly label *all* ancient Jewish sages and rabbis outright Hellenists. In his next sentence, Visotzky allows for such a cautionary qualification by saying, "Many of the rabbis, if not most . . . ." Moreover, one needs to be sensitive to diachronic concerns, as to whether one is speaking about a personality from the early Tannaic or the early Amoraic period. For example, R. Akiba's command of Greek was apparently deficient. See Lieberman, p. 19. In light of the meager evidence that the New Testament has to offer on this subject, I suspect that although Jesus could speak "Street Greek," his rhetorical skills in that language would not have been remarkable.

Did they succeed? Yes, and they should be commended for their great achievement.[13]

The rabbis, and their forerunners the sages, were competing with the Roman circus and amphitheater.[14] This same sort of challenge faces pastors today in promoting biblical literacy among the laity. Indeed, we are competing with the World Wide Web, National Football League, and Music Television, but imagine trying

---

[13]Writing some time near the beginning of the fourth century, the famous church historian Eusebius made a commendatory remark in one of his apologetic treatises about the ability of seasoned Jewish teachers (in contrast to unskilled readers of the text) to delve deeply into the Scriptures and ascertain their essence. The development and mastery of midrashic exegesis played a major role in the rabbis' ability to penetrate and ascertain the essence of the biblical text. For a Greek text of Eusebius' remark, see *Preparation for the Gospel* 12:1 in J. P. Migne, ed. *Patrologia Graecae* (Patrologiae Cursus Completus) (Paris, 1858), p. 952. For an English translation, see Eusebius, *Preparation for the Gospel*, trans. E. H. Gifford (Grand Rapids: Baker, 1981), p. 621. As an interesting aside, see *M. Yoma* 1:6 where two levels of reading Scripture are also mentioned. See also José Faur, *Golden Doves with Silver Dots* (Bloomington: Indiana University, 1986), pp. xviii, 150.

[14]Roman audiences viewed theatrical and dramatic productions in the amphitheater. (Some Roman amphitheaters were fitted out to accomodate gladiatorial contests.) In *Leviticus Rabbah* 11:9, the righteous are described in the world to come as participating in a lively chorus line of dancers and singers. Each of them will point to the lead dancer, who is none other than God himself. The point is that the righteous will be rewarded for having refrained from attending such events. See *Midrash Wayyikra Rabbah*, ed. Mordecai Margulies (New York: Jewish Theological Seminary of America, 1993), pp. 240, 241. For an English translation, see Jacob Neusner, trans. *Judaism and Scripture: The Evidence of Leviticus Rabbah* (Chicago: University of Chicago, 1986), pp. 275, 276.

to coax people into attending a Bible study when in the next town gladiators were battling each other and wild beasts were pitted against men. Israel's spiritual leaders worked hard at dissuading people from attending the *munus gladiatorium* and *venatio*.[15]

The time of flowering for midrash more or less runs from about 100 B.C. to the close of the Byzantine period. The first group of rabbinic, midrashic texts put into writing includes the *Mekilta*, *Sifra*, and the two *Sifre*. This group of written midrashic commentaries circulated in the land of Israel by 200 A.D. These are the Tannaitic *midrashim*, and all of them are commentaries on individual books of the Torah.

After the Tannaitic Period, a second group of rabbinic midrashic commentaries were put into writing by 500 A.D. These later commentaries, compiled and edited between 200 and 500 A.D. in the land of Israel, are called Amoraic *midrashim*. They include *Genesis Rabbah*, *Leviticus Rabbah*, *Pesikta de Rav Kahana*, *Ecclesiastes Rabbah*, *Lamentations Rabbah*, and *Song of Songs Rabba*. Although less pronounced than in the Tannaitic Period, the emphasis again tended to be on passages from the Torah. The close of the Amoraic

---

[15]In *Jewish Antiquities* 15:267-276, Josephus complained about Herod because he had built a theater in Jerusalem and a very large amphitheater in the plain where he hosted Roman games. For an English translation, see Josephus, v. 8 in *The Loeb Classical Library*, trans. Louis Feldman (Cambridge, MA: Harvard University Press, 1963), pp. 127-131. In *Leviticus Rabbah* 13:3, those who refrained from attending wild beast contests will be rewarded in the world to come by admission to the greatest wild beast contest ever: Leviathan will be pitted against Behemoth; see *Midrash Wayyikra Rabbah*, pp. 277, 278. For an English translation, see Neusner, p. 294.

period more or less ended the era of the sages or *hachamin* in Hebrew. In other words, it was the end of the classical period of midrash. Jewish scholars and scribes, however, still collected the comments, sayings, and stories of the *hachamin* and published them in additional works bearing the name "midrash." That is the reason that we can speak about much later mid-rashic collections dating from the 9th century A.D.

Jesus lived in Israel in the first century A.D. Midrash flourished in Israel from about 100 B.C. to A.D. 600. Jesus flourished in the same historical, cultural, and religious context as the sages, the pioneers of midrash. Thus, it is highly probable that he, too, read his Bible midrashically.[16]

Would I be incorrect to say that in Christian seminaries and Bible colleges most of the students would be hard-pressed to describe competently what midrash is? Do we read and preach the Bible the way Jesus read and preached his Bible? This impacts all of us whether or not we choose to think about it.

A third consideration is that the New Testament, for the most part, was written by Jews. Early on, the New Testament jumped cultures from a Jewish culture to a Gentile one. (Emphasis here is primarily on what

---

[16] "An analysis of the exegetical traditions of Ishmael in Tannaitic texts shows that Ishmael . . . most commonly employs the *a fortiori* argument and the *gezerah shawah* . . . ." H. L. Strack and G. Stemberger, *Introduction to the Talmud and Midrash* (Minneapolis: Fortress Press, 1992), p. 24. This remark is germane to the discussion at hand because the same two methods of interpretation are among Jesus' favorites. Moreover, parables stand out as a hallmark literary form of the *midrashim*. The same is essentially true of the synoptic gospels.

happened in Western Christian tradition.) As more and more Gentiles became Christians in the regions of Asia Minor, Greece, Italy, Spain, France, and the British Isles, the Jewish element in the Western Church became less pronounced, and for various historical reasons, it eventually evaporated.

As Christianity spread westward toward Europe, the original Jewish writers of the New Testament remained behind. They did not jump cultures with the text. A new group of readers began reading the New Testament. Besides Jews, who had studied under teachers like the respected Pharisee Gamaliel the Elder, other people who had been schooled as Roman lawyers, rhetoricians, and philosophers began reading the text.[17] Did they see new emphases? Absolutely! When the New Testament jumped cultures, a different audience started to interpret the text, and a new reading of the text with new emphases emerged.

An example of a new emphasis which comes to mind is the Trinity. The word "Trinity" does not appear in the New Testament. It makes its first appearance in Christian literature in the writings of Theophilus of Antioch (ca. A.D. 180). Ample prooftexts can be assembled from Scripture to defend the doctrine of

---

[17]For example, Justin had been trained as a philosopher, Tertullian as a lawyer, and Cyprian as a teacher of rhetoric. Parkes, p. 72. Origen, having been raised and educated in a Christian environment, as an adult achieved command of the works by the Middle Platonists and studied pagan philosophy and literature. *The Oxford Dictionary of the Christian Church*, rev. ed., eds. F. L. Cross and E. A. Livingstone (Oxford: Oxford University Press, 1990), p. 1008.

Trinity. Nevertheless, if Jewish readers in the land of Israel had remained as the stewards of the New Testament, would they have conceived of developing such a doctrine? In order to lead out of the text Trinitarian doctrine, the Bible must be read with a particular accentuation. As one of my favorite teachers at seminary was fond of saying, "The lumber to build the doctrine of Trinity is in the Bible"—if we choose to build it. Of course, this does not negate the doctrine, but it does raise stimulating hermeneutical questions.

What concerns me is how we exegete the New Testament. We have over-directed our attention on its target culture—the greater Hellenistic world—and given insufficient attention to the source culture—Second Temple Judaism. There have always been exceptional Christian scholars who have resisted this trend, such as Jerome,[18] who, in the fourth century, made a real effort

---

[18]Although Jerome's scholarly pursuits were commendable, his attitude toward the Jewish community did not rise above the opinions of other Christian leaders of his day. Their writings reflect an attitude of disparagement. Parkes, pp. 153, 154. In the same vein, Krister Stendahl has remarked, "While bigotry and hatred always exist as an underbrush [in reference to the record of Christian anti-Judaism], Christian contempt for the Jews in its most virulent form is found among some of the greatest figures of the Christian tradition: John Chrysostom, Augustine and--worst of them all, Martin Luther--from whom I have learned such great insights in other respects." Krister Stendahl, "Can Christianity Shed Its Anti-Judaism," *Brandeis Review* (Spring 1992), p. 24. Since the time of its adolescence, Christianity has struggled with its relationship to Judaism. To address this complex subject would be beyond the scope of this essay. Nevertheless, it is within its scope to point out that Christian attitudes toward the Jewish community and its faith profoundly affect the way in which we read our Bible. In an introduction to Elmer

to go back and learn about the Hebraic roots of his Bible and Christianity. Through the centuries, a trickle of learned Christians have dedicated themselves to Judaic studies. One outstanding example of a Christian Hebraicist was Edward Pococke. Late in the 17th century, he penned these words in his commentary on Micah in an opening letter of gratitude to Seth Lord Bishop of Sarum:

> *The concurrence of several reasons, (each of which were sufficient) have moved me to offer to your gracious acceptance this Essay . . . . And thirdly the need of patronage and protection that this Work hath, in regard that there is in it much stress laid on such part of Learning, (the Orientall I mean,) which of late, if not all along, hath had that unhappiness, as to be scarce able to keep it self, not only from neglect, but contempt, as needless; at least of no great use or necessity.*[19]

Josephson's book, David Flusser commented, "The 'Jewish Problem' is not in [the] periphery of Christianity . . . . In reality, the Jewish Problem is one of the central Christian problems: a wrong position toward the Jews means a distorted approach to God and His Word and a misunderstanding of the very claim of the Christian message." Elmer A Josephson, *Israel God's Key to World Redemption* (Hillsboro, KS: Bible Light Publications, 1974), p. 5. Even today too many Christians regard the Old Testament as merely a source from which to extract messianic prooftexts and typologies. As a principal part of the Canon, the Old Testament should be playing a more significant role in the life of the Church. This attitude toward the Old Testament is symptomatic of the "distorted approach" about which Flusser has warned.

[19]Edward Pococke, *A Commentary on the Prophecy of Micah* (England: Oxford University, 1692), n.p.

The "part of Learning" to which Pococke referred as "Orientall" would be called in our day "Judaic Studies." Three centuries ago Pococke expressed similar concern that we have neglected to direct sufficient attention on the source culture of the Christian faith—the Oriental.[20]

---

[20]This tendency can still be seen in seminary curricula across the United States. New Testament Greek is almost always emphasized more in the degree requirements. Two obvious consequences of this policy are: 1) weak integration of Old Testament texts into weekly homilies, and 2) a paucity of Christian Hebraicists to serve such organizations as Wycliffe and the United Bible Societies. This situation could be reversed if the laity were to demonstrate the resolve to initiate change both in the pulpits and in the institutions that educate preachers to fill them.

A DIFFERENT SORT OF BOOK

Allow me to change direction slightly and address some challenges presented by the intrinsic nature of the biblical text.

One challenge is that, because of the popularity of the historical-critical method, most theologically conservative seminary hermeneutics classes focus on the original, historical meaning of a passage. For example, in the case of Isaiah, we ask what a passage meant to the prophet's audience when he first spoke his words. That certainly is an important task to pursue—to assemble all the data which we can glean from archaeology, linguistics, or whatever other discipline, and apply them to the text of Isaiah in order to understand better what a passage meant to his eighth century audience.

Although this interests me, what interests me more is what Isaiah's text meant to Jews in Jesus' day. We are now talking about the historical development of biblical interpretation. Isaiah lived in the eighth century B.C. Jesus lived in the first century A.D. Jesus did not necessarily understand Isaiah's words in the same way which Isaiah's audience understood them. Ideally, we could benefit from two separate tracks of study on the book of Isaiah: what a passage meant to eighth-century B.C. Jews, and what the same passage meant nine centuries later to Jews living in the first century.

A second challenge stems from the fact that the New Testament is a collection of books. These books are diverse in literary form, what scholars refer to as literary genre. As an illustration of the importance of literary form, when watching the evening news, we do not

expect the anchorperson to say, "Once upon a time . . . ."
Literary form tells us how to orient ourselves as we approach a text. A seasoned reader has the sensitivity and
ability to adapt his or her hermeneutic or method of
interpretation to each distinct literary genre of the New
Testament.

A good portion of the New Testament consists of
letters which were written by Paul. Interpreting letters
has its own difficulties. One of them is that we are eavesdropping on a two-way conversation. I have been mar-
ried nine years, during which time I have eavesdropped
on a few of my wife Janet's telephone conversations. I
pretend to be reading but have an ear bent toward the
telephone. Inevitably I get a distorted version of the
conversation because I only heard half of it. Paul's letters present us with a similar sort of challenge. We are
basically eavesdropping on a conversation.[21] On the
surface, the Pauline epistles seem relatively easy to interpret, but in reality they are very difficult, because we
are missing the other half of the dialogue.

Sensitivity to diversity of literary form or genre is a
prerequisite for sound critical biblical interpretation.
The book of Revelation is not a letter, a gospel, nor
historical narrative, but an apocalypse. The literary
genre known as apocalyptic literature has unique features which need to be considered when reading it. The
account of John's vision on the Isle of Patmos must be
read against the backdrop of other apocalyptic texts,
most of which are preserved in the extra-canonical

---

[21]See Jakob Jónsson, *Humour and Irony in the New Testament*
(Leiden: E. J. Brill, 1985), p. 223.

literature of Second Temple Judaism and early Christianity. A representative example of this genre is 2 Esdras, which is found in the Apocrypha and Slavonic Bibles of the Russian Orthodox Church.

MATTHEW, MARK, LUKE, AND JOHN

Another example of a literary genre is the gospel. Matthew, Mark, and Luke belong to the synoptic tradition. The content of these three gospels overlaps to a large extent. This overlap scholars explain in terms of literary interdependence. John, on the other hand, is not part of the synoptic tradition because most scholars think that it is based on distinct sources, is of a different literary form, and does not share heavily in the literary interdependence of the synoptic tradition. A simple analogy for helping to understand the relationship of the gospel of John to Matthew, Mark, and Luke is the relationship of Deuteronomy to Exodus, Leviticus, and Numbers.

Read Exodus, Leviticus, and Numbers carefully, and then read Deuteronomy. Notice the interrelationship of Deuteronomy with those three books. Deuteronomy is a reworking of and supplement to materials found in Exodus, Leviticus, and Numbers. The laws which were given to the nomadic Israelites in the desert now had to be applied to a sedentary agricultural lifestyle in the land.

In Deuteronomy, Moses is depicted giving extended discourses. The same is true of John where Jesus is presented giving long uninterrupted speeches. Deuteronomy, in comparison to Exodus, Leviticus, and Numbers, is a book where historical concerns have shifted to theological concerns. A similar shift has occurred in John. In comparison to the first three gospels, John resembles more a theological than historical presentation of Jesus. *The Oxford Dictionary of the Christian Church* has described John's gospel in this manner:

"It is evidently not a simple account of the Lord's miracles and popular teaching, but a deeply meditated representation of His Person and doctrine by a contemplative conscious of inspiration by the Holy Ghost."[22]

In the synoptic tradition Jesus tells parables. John's gospel preserves no record of Jesus speaking in the classical form of a parable. New emphases also emerge. In John's gospel, Jesus talks frequently about eternal life and believing and less about the Kingdom of Heaven (or Kingdom of God) and doing. The opposite is true of the synoptic tradition. One implication of these observations seems to have been already voiced eighteen centuries ago by Clement of Alexandria. He referred to John as a "spiritual gospel."[23]

Like Luke's gospel, the writer of John disclosed his motives for writing: ". . .but these [signs] have been written that you may believe that Jesus is the Christ, the Son of God; and that believing you may have life in his name" (John 20:31). John's gospel was penned sometime between A.D. 90 and 110. These were hard times for the Christian communities living under the shadow of Roman rule and experiencing the first stages of the rift between the Church and Synagogue. In what was apparently the first conclusion to his gospel, the writer exhorted the reader to believe. That is the main thrust of John's gospel. It serves what we may call a devotional-like

---

[22]*The Oxford Dictionary of the Christian Church*, p. 744. For a simple, helpful introduction to John's Gospel, see the *Saint Joseph Edition of The New American Bible* (New York: Catholic Book Publishing, 1992), pp. 142-144.

[23]Ibid. p. 744.

purpose, presenting Jesus in a manner which encourages us to remain steadfast in the faith.

I have drawn out this discussion of John's gospel because it raises important issues for reading the Book, especially as it pertains to understanding Jesus. In Evangelical preaching, teaching, and writing there is a noticeable favoritism for John's gospel. For example, this comment is found in The Open Bible:

> The Synoptic Gospels read like the hustle and bustle of the marketplace, the action on the highway, and in the crossroads of human commerce. But, in John's Gospel, one has turned into a quiet cathedral, where he is called upon to meditate upon the deep things of the Eternal Son of God.[24]

A second example of favoritism which comes to mind is that recently two young Baptists knocked on the door and handed me a tract entitled "How To Get To Heaven." The tract includes five citations from the gospels, four from John, and one from Luke (John 1:1 and 14, 3:16, 10:28 and Luke 13:3).[25]

The favoritism expressed especially by Evangelicals for John is done unwittingly. I can suggest two reasons for this tendency. One is that John's gospel effectively uses imagery and metaphors which transcend time and place. Twentieth-century Christians marvel at the lofty ideas and truths these images and metaphors carry. The Jesus of the synoptic tradition does not speak with such universal, sweeping metaphorical language. He is more

---

[24]The Open Bible (Nashville: Thomas Nelson, 1979), p. 1010.

[25]"How to Get to Heaven" (Lebanon, OH: Fellowship Tract League, tract no. 153).

31

provincial, and in order to coax out the hard-hitting message of Jesus from the synoptic tradition, a reader must make a real effort to enter Jesus' conceptual world. He or she should be skilled in handling ancient Jewish sources and have a working knowledge of Hebrew and Greek. These skills are the necessary credentials for entering Jesus' conceptual world.

The other reason for favoritism emerges from dealing with the discrepancies in the gospels by instinctively conflating the accounts together in one's mind and producing a mental harmonization of all four. The result is that the gospel with the strongest voice assumes the lead role in molding our perception of Jesus. That gospel is the Gospel of John.

To read the gospels without being aware of or without regard for the distinct features of John's gospel is a step in the wrong direction. John's account is a "deeply meditated representation of His Person and doctrine."[26] Unlike the first three gospels, which have been primarily built from historical snippets of Jesus' life, John's gospel is not a simple account of Jesus' teachings and miracles. Therefore, to read the Fourth Gospel as purely history contributes to displacing Jesus and his message from its authentic historical foundation. At the forefront of Jesus' teachings are the Kingdom of Heaven and doing. Some of us have made an error as pronounced as reading Robert Frost's delightful prose as if it had been excerpted from an issue of *Scientific American*.

---

[26]See footnote 22, p. 30.

WHO NEEDS ORDER?

The synoptic gospels are not really historical narrative. They do not belong to the same literary genre as Acts. The main reason for putting the synoptic gospels in a category other than historical narrative is that although they contain a wealth of excellent historical material, the chronological skeleton in them is artificial.

If we compare Matthew, Mark, and Luke to see where various episodes appear in the life of Jesus, we will find that the order is not consistent. The artificial chronological skeleton resists characterizing the synoptic gospels as historical narrative. Rather than attempting to speculate why the life of Jesus lost its chronological framework, I want to suggest that this development should not necessarily be surprising.

In the prologue to his gospel, Luke actually implied that he had restored some sort of chronology to the story. There he wrote, *"It seemed fitting for me as well, having investigated everything carefully from the beginning, to write it out for you in"* (what type of order?) *"consecutive order, most excellent Theophilus."* Luke has indicated that there has been a disruption in the chronological sequence of the life of Jesus. Because of the thorough investigation he had done, Luke felt qualified to give an orderly account. We are very fortunate he decided to write his account. If we did not have Luke's gospel, we would be in an unhappy situation. Thank God for all of the gospels, but there is a special character to Luke's composition that is so helpful when interpreting Jesus. He had a distinct way of handling his sources and composing his gospel narrative.

33

A quotation from Eusebius, who was the Bishop of Caesarea and a famous church historian, contributes to this discussion. Focus on the issue of the order of the events in the gospels:

> And the Presbyter used to say this, 'Mark became Peter's interpreter and wrote accurately all that he remembered, not, indeed, in order, of the things said or done by the Lord. For he had not heard the Lord, nor had he followed him, but later on, as I said, followed Peter, who used to give teaching as necessity demanded but not making, as it were, an arrangement of the Lord's oracles, so that Mark did nothing wrong in thus writing down single points as he remembered them. For to one thing he gave attention, to leave out nothing of what he had heard and to make no false statements in them.'[27]

Although Mark's gospel is based indirectly on a historical report, the fact that (if we are to trust Papias' claim) he did not record the events of Jesus' ministry in chronological order makes classifying his gospel as a historical narrative difficult. (For the record, I am not convinced of the accuracy of Markan priority. I regard it as a competing synoptic source theory. Because of my training in midrash, when working in the synoptic tradition, I am often drawn to the Lukan narrative in the triple tradition and Matthean-Lukan double tradition texts.)

---

[27]Here in *The Ecclesiastical History* 3:39, Eusebius was quoting from the writings of Papias. Papias (circa A.D. 100) served as the Bishop of Hierapolis in Asia Minor. The above quotation comes from Eusebius, v. 1 in *The Loeb Classical Library*, trans. Kirsopp Lake (Cambridge, MA: Harvard, 1959), p. 297.

From the ancient Jewish sources, we learn that, in the Jewish mind, chronological order was not an absolute priority for giving meaning to a text. That rails against our Western sensibilities, but in ancient Jewish thinking, chronological order, though it had some significance, was not indispensable for giving meaning to a text.

What set this sort of precedent? How could the early followers of Jesus have been content with an account of his life where the chronological skeleton had not been preserved?

Consider Numbers 9:1, where it says, *"Thus the Lord spoke to Moses in the wilderness of Sinai, in the first month of the second year after they had come out of the land of Egypt . . . ."* Turn now to the beginning of the same book: *"Then the Lord spoke to Moses in the wilderness of Sinai, in the tent of meeting, on the first of the second month, in the second year after they had come out of the land of Egypt . . . ."* Which event happened first? Which chapter has priority chronologically? Numbers 9:1 occurred before Numbers 1:1. The nature of the Torah itself set the precedent for chronological order not being an absolute priority for giving a text meaning.

The absence of a consistent chronological order is not a feature restricted only to the Torah. Notice the beginning of Isaiah: *"The vision of Isaiah the son of Amoz, concerning Judah and Jerusalem which he saw during the reigns of Uzziah, Jotham, Ahaz, and Hezekiah . . . ."* Turn now to Isaiah 6:1: *"In the year of King Uzziah's death, I saw the Lord sitting on a throne, lofty and exalted, with the train of his robe filling the temple."* From the pattern reflected in other prophetic books like Jeremiah and Ezekiel, it seems that the call of this prophet in the year of Uzziah's death (Isaiah 6:1-7) occurred before the vision concerning Judah and Jerusalem (Isaiah 1:1-9). Modern critical scholarship endorses this opinion, but before textual criticism ever emerged as a recognized discipline of study, the rabbis of old had concluded the same.[28]

There is a well-known principle in Judaism which says in Hebrew: אין מוקדם ומאוחר בתורה. Literally, this means that there is no earliness or lateness in the Torah. In more dynamic English, we would say that there is no consistent chronological order to events in the five books of Moses.[29]

Along the same line, Rabbi Nehemiah was fond of saying, "The words of the Torah are poor in their place, but rich in another place."[30] His saying provides insight into Jewish methods of interpretation. The ancient sages basically continued what they saw in the Torah. They followed the Torah's lead and began separating and recombining passages. Using concordance-like principles, they did this easily because they had learned the Bible by rote. Two examples of these interpretive methods are *gezerah shavah* and *harizah*. *Gezerah shavah* is an early rabbinic expression that refers to a simple linking of verses based upon the presence of a common word or

---

[28]See *Mekilta de Rabbi Ishmael* on Exodus 15:9 in *Mechilta D'Rabbi Ismael*, ed. H. S. Horovitz and I. A. Rabin (Jerusalem: Wahrmann Books, 1970), p. 139. For an English translation, see Reuven Hammer, trans., *The Classic Midrash: Tannaitic Commentaries on the Bible* (Mahwah, NJ: Paulist, 1995), p. 112.

[29]See David Daube, *The New Testament and Rabbinic Judaism* (New York: Arno Press, 1973), pp. 408-410, 412-417.

[30]*Talmud Yerushalmi, Rosh HaShanah* 3:5, 58d (Krotoschin ed.).

phrase. (Note Luke 10:27 where a lawyer combined Leviticus 19:18 and Deuteronomy 6:5 largely because of the common Hebrew word ואהבת *veahavta* meaning *and you shall love.*) *Harizah* is a later rabbinic term referring to "stringing pearls"—starting with a verse from the Torah, stringing it with one from the Prophets, with a second from the Writings, and back into the Torah again. The end result is that the text is atomized, or chopped up, and the pieces reshuffled. This midrashic activity gives new meaning to the text because reading verses in the light of other verses generates fresh perspective. The sages and rabbis were delighted with the result: the more meaning the better!

As a tangential comment, I will mention that in English translations of the Bible there are places in the legal sections of the Torah which the Bible editors have subtitled "sundry laws." What are sundry laws? A hodgepodge! The modern English speaking editors are saying that this material is so unsystematic, they do not know how to categorize it. In other words, the logic employed by the ancient editors in grouping this material has eluded the grasp of the modern editors. Moreover, this untidy arrangement of material also facilitated the development of such interpretive methods as *gezerah shavah* and *harizah.*

Has anyone encountered places in the synoptic gospels, particularly in Luke, where Jesus jumps from one topic to another, and there is little logical connection between the verses? If the answer to the question is "no," I recommend reading Luke 11:32-36 or 16:16-18. This presents a difficulty in interpreting the synoptic gospels, especially because in seminary we are taught to rely on the context of a verse for proper interpretation. In regard to certain passages in Luke, such normally sound advice may prove misleading.[31]

The initiative of Luke giving consecutive order to the events in the life of Jesus was brought to a logical conclusion with Tatian's work called the Diatessaron in A.D. 160. This was a harmonization of the gospels. Thus, there was an impulse in the early church to reduce the discrepancies between the accounts. By the second century A.D., Tatian had resolved the discrepancies with his arrangement of the four gospels into a continuous narrative. The Diatessaron remained the standard text of the gospels for the Syriac church until the fifth century.[32]

If we compare the table of contents of the Hebrew Bible, which has a different order of contents from that of an English Bible (which has taken its lead from the Septuagint), I think the case could be argued that an impulse toward chronological order is also reflected in the new arrangement of some of the books in the Septuagint.

For whom was the Septuagint translated? Jewish scholars translated most of it from Hebrew to Greek

---

[31]One reason for this is that the nature of the materials that Luke received and reworked did not always allow him to revise and rearrange them successfully into a flowing chronological sequence. At times he had to supplement a chronological principle of editing with other ways of grouping materials. For example, Luke employed catchwords or "stichwords" to give diverse, originally unrelated, materials a cohesiveness. In places where Luke employed "stichwords," relying on the context of a verse may frustrate the exegetical process. For further discussion on this point, see J. W. Doeve, *Jewish Hermeneutics in the Synoptic Gospels and Acts* (Assen, Netherlands: Van Gorcum, 1954), p. 180.

[32]*The Oxford Dictionary of the Christian Church*, p. 400.

for readers in the Hellenistic world. Perhaps in its table of contents we see a trace of an impulse toward chronology becoming more of a consideration for meaning. It seems to be discernible in the arrangement of some of the books.

The ancient Jewish mind in the land of Israel did not demand that a text have a fixed, authentic chronological structure in order to give it meaning, and, therefore, preserving a narrative's original structure may not have been a primary concern. Hellenistic thinking, however, apparently did not feel as comfortable with this proposition.[33] The same is true of modern, critical, rational thinking.

The impulse toward chronologicizing the Bible remains in our day. There is a new *NIV Narrated Bible in Chronological Order*. The promotional statement on the inside leaf of the jacket boasts:

> *Now, an entirely new way to read your Bible! For the first time, you can read the Bible in one of the most understandable and interesting presentations ever. The widely acclaimed New International Version has been chronologically arranged in the order that events occurred.... A complete harmony of the Scriptures....*[34]

---

[33]An early example of concern for accurate chronological reporting in the development of Greek historiography may be seen in Thucydides' account of the Peloponnesian War. Thucydides wrote toward the end of the fifth century B. C. See *History of the Peloponnesian War* 1:97 and 5:26. For an accessible English translation, see his *History of the Peloponnesian War*, trans. Rex Warner (London: Penguin Books, 1972), pp. 93, 363.

[34]*NIV Narrated Bible in Chronological Order* , ed. F. LaGord Smith (Eugene, OR: Harvest House, 1989).

Have not these Christian Bible editors done a similar thing to the text as the rabbis of old? By separating and recombining the text, they have offered the reader "an entirely new way" of reading his or her Bible. I have no doubt that they succeeded in what they set out to achieve.

The reason that I have belabored this point is that working with the scant evidence which is available, I get the impression that the life of Jesus, which evolved into the synoptic tradition, began losing its chronological skeleton while in the context of a Hebrew and Aramaic-speaking, Messianic Jewish community in the land of Israel. After the synoptic tradition had been translated from Hebrew to Greek, an impulse emerged toward restoring the chronological skeleton. In his prologue, Luke has offered us a glimpse of the process toward reconstructing it.

WHAT DENOMINATION WAS JESUS?

Rich diversity characterized Judaism in Israel in the first century. To use a modern analogy, there was a plurality of "denominations," especially prior to A.D. 70. This diversity within ancient Judaism was inherited by the early church. Moreover, the diverse streams of thought, or "denominational" thinking, found expression in the New Testament.

It would be analogous to Jesus entering the world for the first time in our day. Some of his disciples would be Catholic, some Lutheran, some Anglican, some Pentecostal, and so on. After Jesus' death and resurrection his followers would begin writing about him. The Catholic disciple would describe Jesus with discernible traces of his Catholicism, the Lutheran with discernible traces of his Lutheranism, the Anglican with discernible traces of his Anglicanism, and the Pentecostal with discernible traces of his Pentecostalism.

A similar sort of thing happened during the period in which the books of the New Testament were being written. For example, in the synoptic tradition, Jesus does not talk about himself in terms of being a priestly messiah. The New Testament, however, contains one book, namely Hebrews, which does speak at length about Jesus in terms of a priestly messiahship. It seems that its author had in mind a readership embracing ideas which we now know to have been present in streams of thought linked to the Qumran community.[35] These

---

[35]At the end of his important article on this subject, Yigael Yadin concluded, "There could be no stronger appeal to the hearts and

monastic-like Jews living in the desert near the Dead Sea were expecting a messiah of Aaron.[36] From a canonical perspective, we should talk about Jesus as the priestly messiah, but did Jesus prefer speaking of himself this way?

Various groups of Jews in the first century produced diverse texts with distinct emphases. The Jews at Qumran wrote, among other sorts of texts, apocalyptic literature. The sages of Israel who evolved into the rabbis shortly after Jerusalem's demise in A.D. 70. apparently did not display the same degree of keen interest in apocalyptic speculation. Although Jesus used a number of technical terms which appear also in the Qumran scrolls, he did not endorse the general theological orientation of that sect.

Jesus' teachings are not primarily apocalyptic in nature. Using "apocalyptic" here with a popular nuance, I mean that Jesus did not focus on a time in the future when God will suddenly intervene in the world and set things right. Jesus' teachings do possess a pronounced eschatological element (i.e., a definite opinion concerning the great event to come at the end of the age—the coming of the Son of Man). The eschatological element of Jesus' teachings may be summed up in one sentence.

---

minds of people descending from the DSS [Dead Sea Scrolls] Sect than in those metaphors which are abundant and characteristic in the Epistle to the Hebrews." Yigael Yadin, "The Dead Sea Scrolls and the Epistle to the Hebrews," *Scripta Hierosolymitana* 4 (1965), p. 55.

[36]Cf. *The Manual of Discipline* 9:11. For a Hebrew text, see *Die Texte Aus Qumran*, ed. Eduard Lohse (München: Kösel-Verlag, 1986), p. 32. For an English translation, see *The Dead Sea Scrolls in English*, trans. Geza Vermes, 3rd ed. (London: Penguin, 1990), p. 74.

The great and terrible day of the Lord, which is synonymous with the coming of the Son of Man, could be today; therefore, we ought to be always busy with the affairs of the Kingdom of Heaven. Jesus made a similar point using the unpredictable nature of death (cf. Luke 12:16-20).

The Qumran sect was centripetal. Their teachings encouraged an insular mentality. The Sons of Light were commanded to hate the Sons of Darkness whereas Jesus instructed his disciples to love their enemies. His teachings were centrifugal. They forced his disciples outward among the poor, the captive, and the downtrodden, so that they would spread healing, hope, redemption, and love in a broken world. The Pharisees promoted a similar approach in their teachings. Jesus was not a card-carrying Pharisee, but he was close to them in worldview.[37] This rich diversity of Second Temple Judaism naturally flowed into the canonical text of the New Testament. This is important to keep in mind because we must first strive to listen to what Jesus said about himself in the synoptic tradition and then move slowly outward to Acts, James, and the remaining books of the New Testament, where others have spoken about him.

---

[37]Already calling attention to this observation, David Flusser has written, "Talmudic literature remains our principal source for the interpretation of the synoptic Gospels—which proves, to my mind, that Jesus and his followers were nearer to Pharisaic Judaism than to the Qumran Sect." Flusser, p. 24.

Limitations of the Historical-Critical Method

I am a student of the historical-critical method of interpretation but am also aware of its limitations. To ask what a verse of Scripture meant to its original audience is the right place to start.

Especially when reading the New Testament, I am an advocate of the historical-critical method. As Christians, our attention should be directed toward Jesus and his teachings. The historical-critical method remains the most significant contribution of academia for clarifying the words of Jesus. My decision to pursue an advanced degree in midrash was largely motivated by my seminary experience. While a seminarian, I studied hermeneutics, and one of the principal rules that I practiced was to pay careful attention to the original historical and social context. For Jesus, that context was first-century Judaism in the land of Israel. Expertise in midrash is an indispensable skill for a sound historical-critical methodology of the New Testament,[38] and especially for coaxing from the synoptic tradition the more subtle, but no less sublime aspects of Jesus' teachings.

When reading the Old Testament, I become a more circumspect subscriber to the historical-critical method.

---

[38]Geza Vermes has already expressed a similar opinion in these words, "Indeed, without the help of Jewish exegesis it is impossible to perceive any Christian teaching in its true perspective." Geza Vermes, "Redemption and Genesis XXII" in *The Sacrifice of Isaac: Studies in the Development of a Literary Tradition* (Jerusalem: Makor Publishing, 1978), n. p.

I recommend starting with it, but not being restricted to it. An inherent tension exists between the historical-critical approach to biblical interpretation and the concept of Canon. Historical criticism aims at identifying the original, authentic, true meaning of a verse or passage: what did the text mean to the original audience?

In the Old Testament there are many passages which remain outside the scope of the historical-critical method. Sufficient historical, archaeological, and linguistic information to interpret these passages is simply not available. Accordingly, we shy away from these passages in our preaching and teaching, and in the end contribute to the NTB—The New Truncated Bible. (Of course, the NTB also gets assistance from denominations and churches which repeatedly highlight specific verses to uphold doctrine.) If anyone doubts the existence of the NTB, I would encourage that person to record all the verses which he or she hears from the pulpit of a non-lectionary reading church over a 24 month period. I suspect the resulting text would be about the thickness of the Minor Prophets or perhaps less.

The nature of Canon resists our inclination to overlook or suppress certain passages which are difficult to understand, irrelevant for contemporary society, or create friction with our doctrines and dogmas. The pulpits of the community of faith must continually strive to ensure that the entire Canon remains in currency in the minds and the hearts of the laity.

In regard to the Old Testament, four limitations of the historical-critical method come to mind. They are as follows:

1) Teaching from an exclusively historical-critical perspective runs the risk of boring the laity.

Christians must truly enjoy their Bibles in order for teaching to be effective. The rabbis of old were keenly aware of this pedagogic principle. Their midrashic comments contain many humorous elements.

2) Jesus did not read his Bible in a historical-critical manner, but from a midrashic perspective. Although Jesus would have recognized and probably favored the *peshat,* or plain meaning of a text, this is not synonymous with its historical-critical interpretation. This means that our understanding of numerous passages from the Old Testament departs considerably from that of Jesus.

3) Some passages remain outside the scope of the historical-critical method because sufficient historical, archaeological, and linguistic information is lacking.

4) Some passages, which can be understood from a historical-critical approach, have little relevance for twentieth-century Christians living in modern Western society.

When these limitations become a consideration, I am prepared to supplement the historical-critical method with a midrashic-like approach to biblical interpretation, but with an explicit, overarching guiding principle, which I will describe in detail. In essence, I read the Book with a hybrid hermeneutic which is sometimes historical-critical and sometimes midrashic. Some may object and complain that I am not being intellectually consistent or systematic, but being a student of the sages, I have learned to hold in tension competing intellectual positions.

A JESUS-CENTRIC APPROACH

When implementing the midrashic side of my hybrid hermeneutic, I find it helpful to take the lead from Judaism in terms of how Jews read their Bible. Traditional Jews believe that all of the Hebrew Scriptures (the Old Testament) are inspired. When Jews read their Bible, however, they place a weighted emphasis on the five books of Moses. Remember that the earliest *midrashim* serve as commentaries on the Torah or five books of Moses. Only when the Jewish community began to rework the material of the Tannaitic *midrashim* did it begin to produce newer commentaries on other books beyond the Torah. Thus, we can see from the *midrashim*, especially from the Tannaitic Period, that Jewish scholarly energy was aimed towards a specific section of the Bible, namely the Torah. Starting with the Torah, a Jewish expositor then moved out to the Prophets and the Writings. Although I am describing these things in a generalized manner, it is accurate to say that there has been and still is a priority of the five books of Moses in Jewish exegesis. It should come as no surprise to discover that Jesus too weighted his teachings with citations from and allusions to the Torah. A careful reading of the synoptic gospels demonstrates this. For example, we see this tendency in the Sermon on the Mount.

What motivated Jews to place such an emphasis on the five books of Moses? When the prophets after Moses prophesied, they received the *devar Adonai* (word of the Lord). What was the word of the Lord? Nobody really knows. But how did Moses communicate with

God? Face to face. Ancient Jews recognized that no one spoke to God in the way Moses did. He spoke to God face to face like a friend (cf. Exodus 33:11, Numbers 12:8, and Deuteronomy 34:10). For this reason, ancient Jews concluded that there was a qualitative difference in the revelation of the five books of Moses. All of the Bible is inspired, but those passages which came from Moses, out of this unique relationship that Moses had with God, warranted more attention.[39]

We could also legitimately say that the Prophets represent the first layer of commentary on the Torah. The same emphases that we see in the Torah are repeated in the Prophets. The classical message of the Prophets is *Mishpat* and *Tsedek*, which we sometimes translate as social justice: feeding the hungry, clothing the naked, visiting those in prison, defending the orphan, widow, and alien. These concerns are first expressed in the Torah. Of course, the prophets did begin to speak of a

---

[39]C. F. Keil and F. Delitzsch offered an insightful discussion of this subject in their commentary on the Old Testament: "Hence Moses was not a prophet of Jehovah, like many others, not even merely the first and highest prophet, *primus inter pares*, but stood above all the prophets, as the founder of the theocracy, and mediator of the Old Covenant. Upon this unparalleled relation of Moses to God and the theocracy, so clearly expressed in the verses before us, the Rabbins have justly founded their view as to the higher grade of inspiration in the *Thorah*. This view is fully confirmed through the history of the Old Testament kingdom of God, and the relation in which the writings of the prophets stand to those of Moses. The prophets subsequent to Moses simply continue to build upon the foundation which Moses laid." C. F. Keil and Franz Delitzsch, *The Pentateuch*, v. 1 in *Commentary on the Old Testament* (Grand Rapids: Eerdmans, 1975), pp. 80, 81.

future era, but the bulk of their energy was devoted toward addressing their circumstances, the social ills which they saw on a daily basis. They were calling their people back to obedience to God—back to the Torah. They emphasized looking out for one's fellow man, making sure that the stranger, the widow, and the orphan were not exploited or forgotten.[40]

When reading the New Testament, I start with Jesus in the synoptic gospels, and then very slowly move outward, because I want to strive first to understand what Jesus said about himself. Once I feel that I have done the best possible job of comprehending Jesus' words in the synoptic tradition, I begin to move out into the remainder of the New Testament to see what others said about him. I strive to be *Jesus-centric* in the manner that I read, preach, and teach Scripture. Once I identify the emphases that Jesus made in his teachings, I then read those emphases throughout the rest of the Bible, particularly in those places where the historical-critical approach fails to satisfy the demands of Canon. In other words, having identified the emphases of Jesus' teachings, I then bend the biblical text toward them. I make no apology; I bend the text, but when I do, I strive to bend it toward Jesus.

The most basic step in bending Scripture toward Jesus is diligent study in the synoptic gospels to hear afresh what he said about himself. This presupposes serious commitment to learning about Jesus' social, historical, and religious context and to studying the

---

[40]Cf. George Foot Moore, *Judaism in the First Centuries of the Christian Era,* v. 1 (New York: Schocken Books, 1971), p. 239.

relevant languages in order to engage in responsible linguistic, comparative, and textual-critical work.

Our faith is centered around Jesus, but the faith of Jesus was centered around Torah. Thus, we will discover that, as we focus on the teachings of Jesus, we will be forced to direct considerable attention back to the five books of Moses. If we do this, our emphases will be more in line with Jesus' emphases, and our language will reflect more of Jesus' language.

Let me give an example of what I mean regarding Jesus' language. It is quite common in Evangelical circles to talk about being "born again." Talking about being born again represents authentic Christian language. The expression is biblical, but how many times does it appear in the New Testament? Two separate places (cf. John 3:3, 7 and 1 Peter 1:23). How many times does Jesus talk about the Kingdom of Heaven (or Kingdom of God)? Dozens of times. Yet we feel more comfortable saying to people, "You must be born again." We can talk that way, but I am suggesting that the ratio needs to be ten "Kingdom of Heavens" for every one "born again," if we are to pull our language into line with that which is reflected in the synoptic gospels.

One reason that readers of this essay may find its contents refreshing is that they are sympathetic to achievements which are linked to the Charismatic Renewal in the Church. Because of a heightened appreciation for the dynamic role of the Holy Spirit in our day, such Christians are less inclined to place rationalistic or doctrinal limitations on God's redemptive activity. Moreover, they tend to recognize that the fulcrum of their faith rests upon a personal redemptive encounter with God. Thus, while the Bible is of great importance for both the individual and the community of faith, it should not be elevated to a status that belongs exclusively to God. To speak of the message of the Bible as inerrant is one thing, but to suggest that perfect biblical text equals perfect God is a proposition which has the potential to shipwreck faith and repel intellectually honest people from the Church.

Reading the Book foreshadows the need for changes on the scale of a reformation in Charismatic-Evangelical thinking. In my opinion, Christians who are sympathetic to the core ideas championed by the Renewal stand at an advantage to meet the challenges which have been discussed above. Nevertheless, the leaders of the Renewal in our day, with their penchant for inaccurate language and disparagement of formal, academic biblical training, must make efforts to cultivate gifted teachers[41] who will kindle a love for serious, disciplined Bible study among the laity sitting in the pews. Like other

---

[41]To remove any ambiguity on this point, when referring to the cultivation of gifted teachers, I mean that congregations (or individuals) must identify, encourage, and financially support students who will one day serve as Bible teachers and translators in the Christian community. As a young adult, a person with high scholastic aptitude and a desire to teach should be encouraged to acquire academic training in order to realize the full potential of his or her talent. Once a young adult demonstrates the ability, motivation, discipline, and commitment required for long-term graduate level studies, the community of faith (or individuals) must ensure that adequate funding is available to subsidize living expenses and tuition costs. To implement this proposal would be expensive, but not idealistic. Money and resources simply follow priorities. As a closing thought, my favorite classes at university were always made memorable not because of the subject but the teacher.

51

denominations and movements, it too needs a renewed commitment to re-examining Jesus' message in its historical and social context: Judaism of the first century, in the land of Israel.

We will know when these changes have started because at that time the laity will insist that those who preach and teach from our pulpits receive part of their professional training in Israel. The decision to educate pastors in the land of the Bible with exposure to Jewish teachers (as well as Christian teachers with a sensitivity to Judaism) constitutes a crucial step in the process of Christian reading, preaching, and teaching becoming more *Jesus-centric*. Ultimately, such a decision would result in pulling Christian practice more into line with the challenges and responsibilities of accepting Jesus' invitation to discipleship.